The Assassination of Archduke Franz Ferdinand: The History and Legacy of the Event That Triggered World War I

By Charles River Editors

A contemporary illustration depicting the assassination

About Charles River Editors

Charles River Editors provides superior editing and original writing services across the digital publishing industry, with the expertise to create digital content for publishers across a vast range of subject matter. In addition to providing original digital content for third party publishers, we also republish civilization's greatest literary works, bringing them to new generations of readers via ebooks.

Sign up here to receive updates about free books as we publish them, and visit Our Kindle Author Page to browse today's free promotions and our most recently published Kindle titles.

Introduction

Contemporary media illustration depicting the assassination

The Assassination of Franz Ferdinand (June 28, 1914)

"It is nothing." – Archduke Franz Ferdinand after being shot on June 28, 1914

By the 20th century, warfare was nothing new to the European powers, especially when it came to fighting each other. Conflicts had been a mainstay on the European continent for over two millennia. Even after the Napoleonic wars had enveloped Europe in large scale war for nearly 20 years in the 19th century, the Europeans' imperialism continued unabated. It would take the devastation of World War I to shock Europe and jolt the world's superpowers out of their imperialistic tendencies.

After Napoleon and the French were was finally defeated in 1815 by a coalition of European nations, Europe went about their most serious attempt to create peace on the continent. Even before the fighting had ended, most major European powers had been meeting in Vienna and established a congress in 1814. A series of agreements were reached between the coalition and the defeated French to end the fighting.

However, the Europeans continued to conduct business as usual, spending much of the 19th century engaged in imperialism across the world. The natural response of the European nations was to establish alliances that would maintain at least a balance of power. In 1873, German chancellor Otto van Bismarck reached an alliance with Austria-Hungary's despot and the Russian czar. The French signed alliances with Britain and Russia, who had left its previous alliance over tension brought about by Austria-Hungary's intervention in the Balkans. By then, Italy had joined the German alliance.

Although a couple of wars were fought on the European continent during the 19th century, an uneasy peace was mostly maintained across the continent for most of the 19th century after Napoleon. Despite this ostensible peace, the Europeans were steadily conducting arms races against each other, particularly Germany and Britain. Britain had been the world's foremost naval power for centuries, but Germany hoped to build its way to naval supremacy. The rest of Europe joined in on the arms race in the decade before the war started.

With Europe anticipating a potential war, all that was missing was a conflagration. That would start in 1908, when Austria-Hungary annexed Bosnia-Herzegovina in the Balkan Peninsula, drawing it into dispute with Russia. Moreover, this upset neighboring Serbia, which was an independent nation. From 1912-1913, a conflict was fought in the Balkans between the Balkan League and the Ottoman Empire, resulting in the weakening of the Ottoman Turks. After the First Balkan War, a second was fought months later between members of the Balkan League itself.

The final straw came June 28, 1914, when a Serbian assassinated Archduke Franz Ferdinand, the heir to the throne of Austria-Hungary, in Sarajevo, Bosnia. Austria-Hungary immediately issued ultimatums to Serbia. When they declared war on Serbia July 28, 1914, Russia mobilized for war as well. The Germans mobilized in response to Russia on July 30, and the French, still smarting from the Franco-Prussian War, mobilized for war against Germany. The British also declared war on Germany on August 4. Thus, in the span of one week, six nations had declared war, half of which had no interest in the Balkans.

Though nobody can know for sure, it's altogether possible that World War I would have still broken out even if Franz Ferdinand had not been murdered. Regardless of events in the Balkans, Germany was already bellicose, France and Austria were concerned and involved, Russia was outwardly aggressive but also dealing with internal dissatisfaction, Italy was poised on the brink, and Britain was desperate to remain aloof but committed to its continental allies and a host of smaller countries clamoring for independence. Europe was too explosive to be rescued by any but the best of diplomats, if at all.

At the same time, it's important not to underestimate the importance of Franz Ferdinand's assassination. In many respects, it was a momentous occasion, both because of the nationality of the conspirators and the context and manner in which it occurred, as well as the disturbing facts that came to light during the subsequent trial.

The Assassination of Archduke Franz Ferdinand: The History and Legacy of the Event That Triggered World War I chronicles the history and legacy of one of the 20th century's most important events. Along with pictures of important people, places, and events, you will learn about the assassination of Franz Ferdinand like never before, in no time at all.

The Assassination of Archduke Franz Ferdinand: The Event That Triggered World War I

About Charles River Editors

Introduction

Chapter 1: A Troubled Line

The Archduke and his family in 1910

Anyone with even a passing acquaintance of history, and certainly anyone schooled in Europe, knows that one of the leading causes of the outbreak of World War I was the assassination of Archduke Franz Ferdinand of Austria-Este, heir presumptive to the throne of Hungary and often referred to as the Archduke of Austro-Hungary. In truth, as most know, Franz Ferdinand's assassination was merely a *casus belli*, the straw that finally broke the camel's back and ushered in a war that had been on the horizon for years. Although many thought the day would never come, its eventual outbreak came as little surprise to the political and military elites that had been watching the storm gather with increasing concern and attention, unable or unwilling to do anything about it.

One of the most ironic aspects of the entire chain of events is that Franz Ferdinand himself was not a great man. He had no great achievements to his name at the time of his death at the age of 50, either in the political, artistic, or military spheres, and while he was not unpopular, he was not cut to be a monarch that would inspire and awe the masses. His career in the Austrian Army had been unremarkable, with the promotions expected for a member of the royal family taking place as a matter of course despite a lack of active service or particular distinction. Likewise, he had not displayed any particular flair for oratory or capturing the hearts of his people.

By all accounts, he was a decent individual beset with heavy responsibilities who was simply trying to do the best he could. Certainly he was no tyrant, and his death was due to what he represented rather than who he truly was. In fact, as the Italian historian Leo Valiani pointed out, Franz Ferdinand sought ways to avoid tensions with Serbia: "Francis Ferdinand was a prince of absolutist inclinations, but he had certain intellectual gifts and undoubted moral earnestness. One of his projects--though because of his impatient, suspicious, almost hysterical temperament, his commitment to it, and the methods by which he proposed to bring it about, often changed--was to consolidate the structure of the state and the authority and popularity of the Crown, on which he saw clearly that the fate of the dynasty depended... Baron Margutti, Francis Joseph's aide-de-camp, was told by Francis Ferdinand in 1895 and--with a remarkable consistency in view of the changes that took place in the intervening years--again in 1913, that the introduction of the dual system in 1867 had been disastrous and that, when he ascended the throne, he intended to re-establish strong central government: this objective, he believed, could be attained only by the simultaneous granting of far-reaching administrative autonomy to all the nationalities of the monarchy. In a letter of February 1, 1913, to Berchtold, the Foreign Minister, in which he gave his reasons for not wanting war with Serbia, the Archduke said that 'irredentism in our country ... will cease immediately if our Slavs are given a comfortable, fair and good life...'"

Franz Ferdinand was born on December 18th, 1863, in the Austrian town of Graz, the scion of the ancient house of Habsburg-Lorraine, a noble dynasty of several centuries which had contributed a large number of European royalty. His father was Archduke Karl Ludwig of Austria, and his mother was Princess Maria Annunciata of the House of Bourbon-Two Sicilies, an Italian noblewoman. One of Franz Ferdinand's uncles (his father's older brother) was Emperor Franz Joseph I of Austria, while another (his father's younger sibling) was "Emperor" Maximilian I, who was persuaded by Napoleon III to allow a French army to install him as Emperor of Mexico until he was killed by a Juarista firing squad during the subsequent uprising.

Franz Joseph I

Karl Ludwig

Franz Ferdinand's cousin, five years his elder, was the heir to the Austrian Imperial throne, Crown prince Rudolph. Rudolph was the heir to the throne of Hungary in addition to Austria, Bohemia and Croatia, but in 1888, at the age of 30 and already a married man, Rudolph met Baroness Marie Vetsera, a 17-year-old noblewoman, and began a passionate and overt affair with her at Mayerling Castle. Franz Joseph I, scandalized by this flagrant disregard for marital piety (although allegedly no saint himself), demanded that his son end his relationship, but rather than give up his newfound love, Rudolph shot her and then himself in an apparent suicide pact in January 1889.

This tragic incident changed the course of Franz Ferdinand's life, and perhaps European history, for good. As eldest living brother and thus heir of Franz Joseph, Karl Ludwig would have been expected to inherit the throne of Hungary, but due to his age, he chose to bequeath the succession rights to his son. Thus, at a stroke, Franz Ferdinand became heir presumptive to the throne of Hungary, although he undoubtedly would not have wanted it to happen under such unfortunate circumstances.

The death of Rudolph marked a watershed moment in Franz Ferdinand's life. Prior to his cousin's death, the young nobleman had been happy to lead a life of leisure, something that had been aided by the fact that at age eleven he had been the recipient of the inheritance of his cousin on his mother's side, Duke Francis of Modena. This had made him one of the richest men in the whole of Europe. He had devoted himself, as expected of a member of the Royal family, to a career in the armed forces, receiving his first commission as a Lieutenant in the Austrian Army at age 14. He was promoted rapidly thereafter, retiring as a Major General at age 31, despite receiving no formal staff training, and retained a professional interest in military affairs up until his death, sitting on military commissions and receiving the appointment of Inspector-General of the Armed Forces the year before his death, in 1913.

Personal tragedy continued to dog Franz Ferdinand for the next few years, with his father dying in 1896 and his aunt, the Empress Elisabeth, murdered by an Italian anarchist two years later. Furthermore, like his cousin Rudolph, Franz Ferdinand's personal life was marked by a turbulent love affair which drew the ire of Emperor Franz Joseph I. In 1894, at the age of 19, he met Countess Sophie Chotek at a formal reception in Prague. Sophie was an aristocrat, but not of the highest caliber, so she was technically ineligible to marry a member of the Royal House of Habsburg since they were required to marry only heiresses from a current or former European ruling dynasty.

Herzogin von Hohenberg
Gemahlin des oesterreichischen Thronfolgers
† 28. Juni 1914.

Sophie

However, Franz Ferdinand, who by all accounts was a deeply passionate, fiery individual, refused to let this courtly constraint daunt him. The two of them evidently cared very much for one another, as evidenced by the letters which Sophie sent Franz Ferdinand when he was convalescing from a bout of tuberculosis on one of the Adriatic islands prior to their marriage. The two of them pursued a semi-secret courtship, with Franz Ferdinand ostensibly visiting the castle where Sophie held the position of lady-in-waiting to an Arch-Duchess, but it was quickly discovered. Franz Joseph confronted Franz Ferdinand over the relationship, complaining that it was unsuitable, and the two of them quarreled bitterly, but Franz Ferdinand refused to end his liaison.

Franz Joseph was certainly influenced by the terrible end his son had suffered, but he refused to see reason for years, despite the intervention of a host of exalted figures, including the

Emperor of Russia, Germany's Kaiser Wilhelm, and even the Pope himself. Many were concerned that such an overt and violent quarrel between members of the Austrian royal family, coming as it did at a time when the Austrian Empire was particularly volatile, could cause deep internal dissent. Indeed, the quarrel between Rudolph, a pro-Hungarian, and his father, a pro-Austrian, had led to dissent already. Eventually, in 1899, Franz Joseph realized that his nephew would never be dissuaded and agreed to let him and Sophie marry, on condition that none of Franz Ferdinand's rank and privileges pass to either Sophie or any of the children they might have. The couple agreed, and they were married in 1900 in the town of Reichstadt.

The strictures of court precedence caused the couple significant strain. For example, at any official function, Sophie had to let senior female aristocrats have precedence, and whenever the royal family was assembled, she was forced to stand far aside with the lesser nobility while other men had their brides with them. Nonetheless, the couple was very much in love. The two of them had three children and stayed committed to one another up until their deaths together in 1914. In a twist of tragic irony, it was their commitment to each other that was partially responsible for their death; Franz Ferdinand's only chance to be seen with his wife publicly was when he was acting in his capacity as Military Inspector, which is one of the reasons he chose to inspect the Bosnian Army in Sarajevo in 1914.

In addition to Sophie, Franz Ferdinand's other great love was travel. He wandered the world extensively both before and after his marriage, including visiting Australia and the Far East on a game-hunting trip in 1893. He subsequently stopped in Borneo, Papua New Guinea, China and Japan before sailing across the Pacific to Canada and then overland across North America before taking ship for the Mediterranean back home. Military and government commitments prevented him from indulging his passion as extensively later in life, but in 1913, he and Sophie embarked on a European tour, the final aim being to visit England, where they were received by the Royal Family, George V and Queen Mary, at Windsor. The couple then traveled to Welbeck Abbey, where they were hosted by the Duke of Portland, who they had met at court.

At Welbeck, Franz Ferdinand went on a shooting expedition with the Duke, and as was customary at the time, their guns were carried by loaders, who would then load them when the game was in sight and hand them to the sportsmen. The ground was muddy and slick with ice, and as the party was preparing, one of the loaders slipped and fell. When the double-barreled shotgun he was carrying hit the ground, it discharged both cartridges, but the shots passed between Franz Ferdinand and the Duke of Portland harmlessly. This close call led the Duke to speculate in later years what might have occurred if the loader had struck Franz Ferdinand.

Ultimately, the picture that emerges from contemporary sources of Franz Ferdinand is that he was a deeply passionate and fiery individual who was curious and well-informed about the world and equally committed to his wife and to the duties thrust upon him as heir presumptive. That passion was not always a positive force, as it sometimes led him to bouts of rage, and likewise, his political opinions displayed a remarkable combination of the nuanced and the unreasonable. Of the Hungarian Magyar patriots and the nascent Hungarian independence movement, he was scathing to the point of xenophobia, describing them as a rabble and dismissing their desires for greater political power out of hand as a direct threat to the hegemony of the Austro-Hungarian Empire. On the other hand, he was a staunch believer in the need for a nuanced approach to handling the potentially explosive situation in Serbia, where grumbles of discontent and feelings of Balkan supremacy risked breaking out into all-out war. This was in direct contrast to the policy of many senior officials in the Austrian army, yet it would be Franz Ferdinand who paid the ultimate price. That said, he was also believed to favor the creation of a third "Slavic" kingdom within the Austro-Hungarian Empire, which would lump many of the Eastern territories together under one crown as a counterpoint to the newly aggressive Serbia. It was this policy that was at least partly responsible for Serbian nationalists singling him out for assassination.

Chapter 2: A Powder Keg Waiting for a Spark

In order to fully understand the implications and motivation for Franz Ferdinand's assassination, it's necessary to understand the situation in Serbia and the Balkans as a whole, and why a small region whose chief importance in the previous centuries had been as a battleground for the great powers to control access to Europe became responsible for the outbreak of World War I. Three years after Franz Ferdinand's birth, in 1878, the Great Powers signed the Treaty of Berlin, a document intended to pacify the Balkans, where the Ottoman Empire had been forced to use brutal force to suppress rebellion on more than one recent occasion. Among other clauses, the Treaty empowered the Austro-Hungarian Empire to take nominal charge of the Bosnia District of the Ottoman Empire, although it officially remained Turkish territory. At the same time, the Treaty also acknowledged the sovereignty of the Principality (later the Kingdom) of Serbia, under the aegis of King Milan Obrenovic, whose family was closely connected to Emperor Franz Joseph's and was well-liked at court. This diplomatic connection helped ensure stability within a notoriously volatile region; administrative power passing to a European power with a Christian government and a long-term vested interest in the East helped quell much of the turmoil to which the Balkans had been subject to under Ottoman rule, while Serbia provided a useful and friendly bulwark to calm any unrest which might occur.

King Milan I of Serbia

However, things went disastrously awry in 1903 when a military coup took place in Serbia. A group of officers and soldiers, commanded by Dragutin Dimitrijević, assaulted the Royal Palace under cover of darkness. After brutal room-to-room fighting, they managed to capture General Laza Petrovic, commander of the Royal Bodyguard, who had escorted the royal family to the safety of a hidden "panic room" while his soldiers held off the attackers. Petrovic was tortured by Dimitrijević and his co-conspirators until he eventually revealed the location of the room's hidden door. The conspirators forced Milan and his wife to open the door, and greeted them with a murderous volley when they did so, continuing to discharge their weapons into their corpses after they had fallen to the ground. The bodies were then stripped and virtually cut to pieces with sabers and bayonets before being hurled from one of the palace windows. A later autopsy concluded that the King had been 30 thirty times and the Queen nearly 20.

Драгутин Т. Димитријевић-Апис

Dimitrijević

  The conspirators then made a clean sweep of it, killing Petrovic before Vojislav Tankosic, Dimitrijević's right-hand man, had the Queen's brothers put to death. Peter Karadordevic was then brought in as the new ruler of Serbia. Karadordevic was a virtual opposite of Obrenovic, which is unsurprising given the circumstances that led to his installation as a monarch, and as a result, Austria no longer benefitted from a friendly power in the Balkans. Instead, it now had a bellicose, fractious, nationalistic neighbor far more interested in cultivating diplomatic ties with Russia than maintaining stability in its home region.

Tankosic

It was Karadordevic's avowed intention to restore Serbia to its medieval glory, when the country had controlled much of the Balkans. This brought Serbia to the brink of open war in 1908, when Austria, desperate for stability in the region, annexed Bosnia-Herzegovina and took it under its own direct administrative and bureaucratic control. Serbia was bellicose, but Austria was a great power, so the Serbians were forced to make the best of it at the time. Karadordevic then turned his attention southwards, where easier pickings could be had, and in 1912 began the Balkan Wars, which ended in 1913 with Serbia's conquest of Kosovo and Macedonia and the defeat of Bulgaria and the Ottoman Empire.

Victory in the Balkans in territories over which Austria-Hungary was supposed to have significant influence emboldened the Serbian military and the even more aggressive Balkan nationalists, who began an aggressive anti-Austrian campaign. Serbia funded rabble-rousers to inflame revolt and dissatisfaction throughout Austria's southeastern territories, and in addition to this, the Serbian secret police also began funding, training and equipping "lone wolf" assassins living within the Austro-Hungarian borders and encouraging them to target officials of the Empire. Although this campaign was largely unsuccessful, it provided further diplomatic strains between the two countries.

Given what would ultimately occur, the most significant of these lone wolves was Bogdan Zerajic, a Serbian student of Law at the University of Zagreb. Zerajic had been chafing for years at the draconian policies enacted by General Marijan Varesanin, the military governor of Bosnia-Herzegovina, who after the 1908 annexation had been employed in a policy of brutal suppression of Bosnian independence movements (likely also partly funded by Serbian intelligence). On June 15, 1910, Zerajic waited for General Varesanin to exit a building to his waiting car and, armed with a revolver, took five shots at him before turning the weapon on himself and using it to shoot himself in the head to avoid capture. Although Zerajic completely bungled the assassination attempt, he became a popular cult figure among anti-Austrian patriots, not least because of his supposedly noble self-sacrifice. Among the many he inspired was Gavrilo Princip, a fellow Serb student and the future assassin of Franz Ferdinand, as well as several of his co-conspirators. Princip idolized Zerajic to an unhealthy degree, reportedly spending whole nights by Zerajic's tombstone in vigil and persuading himself to follow his example.

Varesanin

Zerajic

A state of unease and tension continued to reign between Serbia and Austria-Hungary for the next few years. By the end of 1910 General Varesanin had crushed the Bosnian independence movement apparently for good. However, the situation was still tense as late as 1913, when Franz Ferdinand, in his newly established capacity as Inspector General of the Austro-Hungarian Armed Forces, was ordered by his uncle to visit Bosnia. There he was to inspect the military maneuvers of the Bosnian Army, before proceeding to Sarajevo, where he would preside with his wife over the opening of a new museum of the Bosnian state.

The tension in the Balkans, where by 1913 the Ottoman Empire's holdings had been reduced to the point of non-existence in the wake of Serbian, Bulgarian, Greek, Montenegrin and newly independent Albanian expansion, was symptomatic of what was occurring in Europe as a whole. In the briefest of terms, by 1900 there existed in Europe an interconnected series of alliances, treaties and pacts, both overt and secret, that were intended to maintain the balance of power and the status quo on the mainland, the likes of which had never been seen before. The purpose of this web of alliances was ostensibly to ensure peace, but in reality it meant that an aggressive power could wage small-scale wars with virtual impunity thanks to the looming threat of a full-scale escalation on the European mainland, as had occurred during the Schleiswig-Holstein Question and the Franco-Prussian War (both conflicts started by what was now Germany).

The first of these alliances emerged in the wake of the Napoleonic Wars with the creation of the Holy Alliance, a "triumvirate" of Austria, Russia and Prussia. 60 years later, Otto von Bismarck, perhaps the greatest politician of his age (and certainly the most effective champion of the Prussian cause), created the *dreikaiserbund*, the League of the Three Caesars, a re-affirmation of the previous alliance renegotiated to include Germany. Fittingly, this alliance fell apart over the Balkans, as Russia and Austria-Hungary were at odds over how to administer and exert influence across the region. Thus, in 1879, Germany and Austria-Hungary dropped Russia as a partner to form the Dual Alliance, and three years later, Austria set aside its differences with Italy, which had recently fought two viciously contested wars of independence against Austria to achieve sovereignty. Together, these three nations formed the Triple Alliance.

Bismarck

Things held together (albeit in an extremely fragile fashion) until roughly 1890, shortly after the ascension to the throne of Germany of Kaiser Wilhelm II. Wilhelm was concerned about the vast and shadowy power still wielded by Bismarck, so he compelled Bismarck to resign out of fear that he would undermine the legitimacy and power of the German monarchy by being the de facto ruler. This was a legitimate fear given that the diplomatic circles of Europe still contacted

Bismarck over matters of international policy thanks to their decades-long familiarity with him. What Wilhelm failed to take into account was just how much Bismarck had wielded his personality, ruthlessness, personal magnetism and sheer diplomatic brilliance to keep Germany safe and ensure its constant expansion despite the minefield of European politics. With Bismarck gone, the fragile, informal diplomatic ties he had maintained disintegrated, and in 1890 the Kaiser committed a serious political blunder by refusing to renew the Re-Insurance Treaty, which guaranteed mutual non-aggression between Russia and Germany. Russia then went on to sign the Franco-Russian Alliance with France in 1902, effectively hemming in Germany between two largely hostile powers. France also signed a treaty with Britain, the Entente Cordiale, and in 1907 Britain involved itself further in European affairs by signing the Anglo-Russian Convention. These were not formal alliances, but for simplicity's sake, this complex Anglo-Russian-French arrangement is usually referred to as the Triple Entente. While there were no formal guarantees that Britain would intervene if either France or Russia were attacked or went to war, they certainly strengthened the possibility that this would occur.

Matters in Europe were further complicated by the massive escalation of an arms race. In the wake of the Franco-Prussian War of 1871, Germany had established itself as the dominant power in Europe, and German industrial output had grown by orders of magnitude. By the dawn of the 20th century, Germany was even competing with the mighty Royal Navy for domain over the world's oceans, an impressive output for a country that had never truly made naval power a priority. The *Kaiserliche Marine*, with its modern destroyers, worried the British so much that in 1906 they launched HMS *Dreadnought*, the most powerful battleship of its time. This race for technological supremacy was as much saber-rattling as it was a genuine policy to ensure sufficiently modern equipment in fear of an attack by another European great power, but regardless, military spending almost doubled among most of the powerful nations. Moreover, virtually all nations adopted new breech-loading bolt-action rifles to go along with new artillery pieces, heavy and super-heavy mortars and railway guns, machine guns, grenades, poison gas shells, and a host of other instruments of destruction.

As a result, weapons were becoming deadlier and more powerful just as nations like Germany and Italy were following burgeoning imperialistic agendas, and just as the British and French sought to prevent their expansion. The situation was incredibly volatile, and by 1914, all that was needed was a spark.

Chapter 3: Lighting the Fuse

Much of what is known about the events leading up to the assassination of Franz Ferdinand, and of the conspirators directly involved, is the result of evidence given by witnesses at the trials in 1914 and 1917, including by the conspirators themselves. As always, and particularly given the circumstances of the second trial (which is discussed further below), it's important to scrutinize the legal documents, but with that said, there is every indication that much of what was recorded was genuine because the conspirators had little to hide. Indeed, many of them were quite happy to become martyrs for their cause, and they wanted the world to know in detail what had happened and why.

It all began sometime in 1913 with the Black Hand. This ominously named secret society was a Serbian organization sworn to re-establish the dominance of Serbia to its 14th century imperial grandeur, mostly at the expense of Austria-Hungary. Its methods were murder, sabotage, and terrorism, and among its chief exponents were Colonel Dragutin Dimitrijević, now head of Serbian Military Intelligence, and his right-hand man Major Vojislav Tankosic. It was these two men who had murdered and defiled the corpses of the King and Queen of Serbia and installed Karadordevic as King.

The seal of the Black Hand

In 1913, Dimitrijević, in his capacity as head of Military Intelligence, met with Danilo Ilic, the commander of the Black Hand cell in Sarajevo, Bosnia, in his office in Belgrade. Ilic, a prominent figure in the Black Hand despite not being involved in the Serbian Coup, was an advocate of direct action, and he argued his case strenuously with Dimitrijević. The Black Hand in Bosnia, he argued, was now established sufficiently to allow its members to successfully target the Austro-Hungarian infrastructure. Precisely what Dimitrijević and Ilic discussed is not known, but shortly thereafter, Tankosic met with a number of Black Hand members at a safehouse in Tolouse. Among those summoned by Tankosic was Muhammed Mehmedbasic, a Herzegovinian Muslim who had been recruited to the Black Hand some years previously by Ilic himself, as well as Vladimir Gacinovic, the chief of the Black Hand in Bosnia Herzegovina.

Ilic

Mehmedbasic

At the meeting, Mehmedbasic was informed he would act as an assassin for the Black Hand, a
role that he was only too eager to fulfill. Although a number of names was suggested (including
Franz Ferdinand), the Black Hand ultimately decided that Mehmedbasic should kill Oskar
Potiorek, the Austro-Hungarian governor of Bosnia, in Sarajevo. The Black Hand might have
been shadowy and menacing, but this operation was incredibly amateurish, and Mehmedbasic
proved to be both a bungling and unlucky assassin. Armed with a dagger and a vial of poison, he
boarded a train from France, intending to travel by rail across Europe to Bosnia, but on the way
the train was boarded by the police, who were searching for a thief believed to have jumped on at
the last station to escape capture. Mehmedbasic, believing they were out to get him, jettisoned
his weapons out of the train window. It was only after he had done so and the police searched his

compartment that he realized his mistake, which forced him to search for new weapons in Bosnia. Perhaps concerned about Mehmedbasic's ability to pull the murder off, the Black Hand decided to scrap the whole plan, and Mehmedbasic was recalled to Mostar by Ilic, where they met on March 26th. It was then that Mehmedbasic was told by Ilic that the objective of their operation had changed. It was now Archduke Franz Ferdinand.

Potiorek

It was Dimitrijević who selected the new target, not as a leader of the Black Hand but acting in his official capacity as head of Serbian Military Intelligence. In essence, this meant that the Serbian government and Karadordevic were almost certainly aware of the planned assassination if not directly involved in the plot. Furthermore, both the Russian Ambassador to Serbia and the Military Attachè at the Russian embassy were fully aware of the plot, and they had given it their approval.

Murdering the Archduke of Austria-Hungary, nephew of the Emperor himself and Inspector General of the Austrian Imperial Armed Forces, was obviously far different than murdering the Governor of Bosnia. As important as the latter individual was, targeting Franz Ferdinand required a plan that went beyond the scope of a single lone wolf assassin. For this reason, Ilic set about, on Dimitrijević's orders, recruiting more disaffected young men who could be persuaded to risk – and lay down – their lives for the cause of Serbian triumph and Balkan independence. Shortly after Easter 1914, Ilic recruited Cvjetko Popovic and Vaso Cubrilovic to the Black Hand. The organization also received an unexpected windfall shortly thereafter, when Major Tankosic was notified by one of his subordinates that he had been approached by three Bosnian Serbs, all with family in Sarajevo but living in Belgrade, who wished to give their active support to the cause. These were Trifko Grabež, Gavrilo Princip, and Nedelijko Čabrinović, the erstwhile worshipers of Zerajic.

Grabež, Čabrinović and Princip in Belgrade in May 1914

The young men might have joined with stars in their eyes and the expectation of cloak-and-dagger deeds of derring-do, but the next few months consisted of nothing but boredom and inaction. Tankosic's subordinate kept delaying them, to their intense frustration, and at one point it appeared as though the operation had been called off entirely when it was rumored that Franz Ferdinand had cancelled his Bosnia visit. Eventually, Tankosic got the ball rolling by providing the would-be assassins with a single Fabrique Nationale Model 1910 semi-automatic pistol. Its .380 ACP rounds were hard to come by, so the conspirators could only take a few pot shots each on the outskirts of Belgrade as their marksmanship practice. None of them had been properly trained in its use.

On May 26, 1914, Grabež, Princip and Čabrinović received a further consignment of weapons, including four new Model 1910s with sufficient ammunition for both target practice and action, six hand grenades, a cache of funds, and cyanide pills for them to take in the event of capture. Along with the weapons came Tankosic, who provided training, maps of Sarajevo with the likely points of concentration and police patrols, and perhaps most importantly, details about a secret route which the Black Hand used to smuggle weapons and operatives into Austria-Hungary.

On May 28, Princip, Čabrinović and Grabež journeyed up the Sava River by boat and disembarked at Sabac, where they were met by a Captain Popovic, commander of the Serbian Border Police post there. Popovic directed them onwards by rail under the guise of customs officials to Loznica, a small town on the border between Serbia and Austria-Hungary.

The three were co-conspirators, but that did not make them friends, and by all accounts, Čabrinović was incompetent. He had a violent falling-out with Princip and Grabež at the Border Police office in Loznica, where the two of them forced Čabrinović to hand over his weapons. They gave him Grabež's ID card and told him to make tracks for Zvornik, where he was to cross the border like a regular traveler before meeting with the other two conspirators in Tuzla.

On May 30th, a sergeant of the Serbian Border Police, Budivoj Grbic, agreed to take charge of Princip and Grabež, and he led them on foot to an island in the middle of the Drina River, which formed part of the border between Serbia and Austria-Hungary. They reached the island on May 31 and were handed over to members of the People's Defence, a Serbian nationalist secret society. From there, they travelled in secret over the border to Tuzla, where they arrived on June 3, apparently with the collusion of Major Kota Todorovic, Director of Serbian Military Intelligence on the frontier line. Documents relating to the conspirators' movements during this period were ultimately captured by the Austrian police, and they made clear that the Serbian Prime Minister, Nikola Pasic, was also aware of the plot.

While the three would-be-assassins were waiting for their train in Tuzla, Čabrinović ran into a colleague of his father's, Detective Ivan Vila of the Sarajevo Police, who was also travelling back to the city by train. Čabrinović struck up a conversation with him on the train and discovered that Franz Ferdinand was due to visit Sarajevo on June 28. For the assassins, this was a surprising and fortunate coincidence because June 28th, or Vidovdan to the Serbs, was the anniversary of the Battle of Kosovo, when in 1389 the Serb army had defeated a large force of

Ottoman Imperial troops. Not only did the Serbs win a great victory, but a lone assassin snuck into the Sultan of Turkey's tent and murdered him as he slept. As a result, the day had become symbolic of Serbian independence and patriotism, and being given the chance to assassinate a foreign oppressor on such an auspicious day must have seemed like a good omen to the conspirators.

The trio reached Sarajevo on June 4 and dispersed as agreed. Čabrinović moved in with his father, Grabež went to live with his family in the suburb of Pale, and Princip, after visiting his own relatives in the nearby town of Hadzici, returned to Sarajevo and installed himself with Ilic in his mother's house. On June 14, Ilic himself travelled back to Tuzla, where the trio had stashed their weapons, and brought them back to Sarajevo, concealing them in a box of sugar and changing multiple trains to avoid detection before concealing the weapons in his mother's house.

After this, it becomes unclear what happened next, and the court documents do little to clarify. In his testimony, Ilic gave a contradictory account of what transpired, but it seems that he traveled to the nearby town of Brod and then returned to town. It may have been the case that Ilic had received information that he was to call off the assassination, or that he was first told to abort the mission but then told that it was on again.

Whatever occurred in the period between June 14 and June 28, one thing is for sure: the assassination was not called off. On June 27, the conspirators met in a cafe, where Ilic introduced Princip, Grabež and Čabrinović to the two men he had recruited in Sarajevo (Popovic and Cubrilovic). He also introduced them to Mehmedbasic, who was still in Sarajevo hoping to redeem himself after his botched attempt at murdering Potiorek. Between the six of them, they had a grenade each, five Model 1910 pistols and some spare ammunition, and their cyanide pills. Their plan was simply to attack the Archduke's motorcade as it passed them or when it stopped, ideally in a place where, as per their maps, there was little police presence other than those officers guarding the route. If they struck with sufficient speed and determination, they figured they would be able to shoot Franz Ferdinand dead or destroy his vehicle with a grenade. Getting away clean was desirable but not essential; they were happy to be martyred, hence the cyanide pills. Ilic, on the other hand, took care not to place himself in harm's way. He was an organizer, not a footsoldier.

The Archduke and Sophie at Sarajevo Station on June 28

June 28, 1914, the Feast of St Vitus, dawned clear and cloudless. Shortly after sunrise, Franz Ferdinand, Sophie, and their entourage and bodyguard caught a train from the spa resort of Ilidza, where they had been resting after attending the maneuvers of the Bosnian Army. They arrived in Sarajevo after a short journey, where they were met by a motorcade of six open-topped vehicles and Governor Oskar Potiorek, who had unwittingly been spared assassination at Mehmedbasic's hands. The first vehicle was occupied by the commander of the special security detail assigned to Franz Ferdinand, but due to the confusion that ensued in getting everyone stowed away aboard their respective vehicles, three officers of the Sarajevo Police, rather than the special security detail, got into the car itself, leaving the special officers stranded at the station. The second car was occupied by the Chief of Police and the Mayor, while the third, the most luxurious, was reserved for Franz Ferdinand, Sophie, the Governor, and a senior military official, Lieutenant Colonel Franz von Harrach. The motorcade then took off for the nearby barracks, which Franz Ferdinand was to inspect before proceeding along the river to the Town Hall. Unlike similar visits before and since, there was no army presence and no soldiers or police officers lining the route the motorcade was expected to take, as it was believed that the local citizens of Sarajevo would take their presence as an insult. This was a major security lapse, particularly since the Sarajevo police, which was expected to protect the route, was a skeleton force significantly less than 100 strong.

Picture of the car Franz Ferdinand and his wife rode in on June 28

The Archduke and Sophie in the car on June 28

The first of the conspirators the motorcade passed were Cubrilovic and Mehmedbasic, but while they were dedicated to the cause, neither man had displayed a particular aptitude for espionage or assassination. Mehmedbasic in particular was virtually a liability, as evidenced by how he had panicked on the train to Sarajevo and ditched his weapon because he thought the police were after him. As the Archduke passed them, Cubrilovic was armed with a Model 1910 and a hand grenade, and Mehmedbasic was equipped with a grenade, but for whatever reason – fear, lack of nerve, a change of heart, or a combination of them – they watched the convoy go past without lifting a finger.

Further down the convoy's route was Čabrinović, who was equipped with a hand grenade close by the bank of the Miljacka River. Brash and a braggart with little regard for operational safety, Čabrinović was as ready for action as a man could be, and he had partially redeemed himself from his irresponsible behavior traveling with Princip and Grabež by obtaining details about the date of Franz Ferdinand's visit. When the motorcade approached Čabrinović's position, he pulled the pin on his grenade and hurled it at the car, trying to land it in the bed of Franz Ferdinand's convertible. By a stroke of good luck for the Archduke (at least momentarily), the grenade missed by inches and instead bounced off the folded-up roof of the convertible. A couple of seconds later, the grenade went off under the fourth car, disabling it and wounding the occupants, including the Governor's aide, Erich von Merrizzi. Pieces of shrapnel from the grenade itself, as well as the shredded underside of the car, blew sideways at ankle height, wounding over a dozen people but none of them severely.

Čabrinović hung around long enough to see that his attempt had failed, and then he sprinted for the river. Čabrinović swallowed his cyanide pill, but instead of killing him, it provoked a violent series of stomach cramps as his body rejected it and he vomited the poison up. In desperation, he sprinted for the river and dived in, but he did not know that the Miljacka had been depleted by summer drought and was barely a foot deep. He splashed about in the shallows for a few instants, writhing in agony from the poison and trying to drown himself in the few inches of water, before the police jumped in after him and dragged him onto the bank, where he was beaten half to death by the vengeful crowd before being hauled off to a cell.

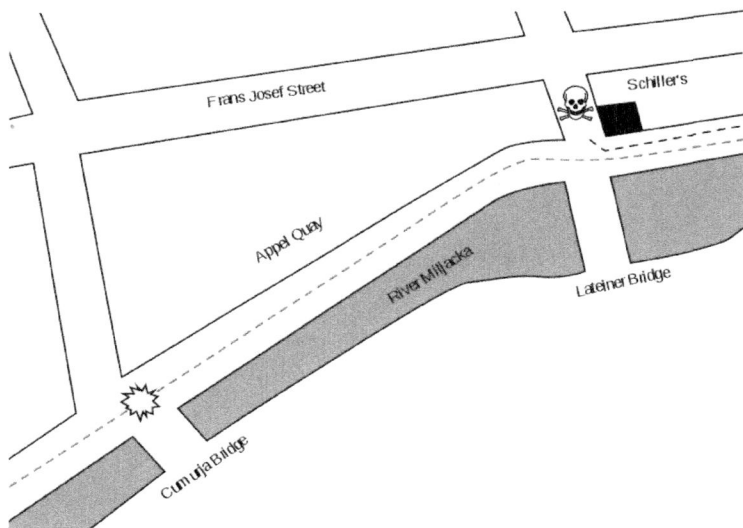

A map of the location of the botched attempt

Despite the botched attempt, the motorcade resumed its progress and headed for the Town Hall while leaving the scuppered car in their wake. The cars now moved at higher speeds to prevent any further attempts, and Popovic, Princip and Grabež watched them go by, powerless to intervene. They had heard the explosion but didn't know if Franz Ferdinand was still alive or not. By the time he was close enough for them to verify he was alive, it was too late to act.

A picture of the Archduke's car arriving at Town Hall after the botched assassination attempt

As noted earlier, Franz Ferdinand had a notoriously ferocious temper, and his mood was not in the least ameliorated by having a hand grenade lobbed at his car. Once they reached the Town Hall, the Mayor, with remarkable aplomb, attempted to carry on with the speech that had been prepared for the occasion, but Franz Ferdinand railed at him, complaining that he had come to visit the city in good faith and had been received not with cheering but with bombs. It was Sophie who rescued the situation by stepping in on the distraught mayor's behalf and whispering something in her husband's ear, after which he let the Mayor continue his speech. Franz Ferdinand then stood patiently by as the Mayor finished his speech, and he then waited until the text of his own was brought to him. Incredibly, Franz Ferdinand's speech was still wet with blood from one of the occupants of the fourth vehicle, and as he delivered his speech, he added some twists of his own, such as the fact that he was proud of the citizens of Sarajevo for greeting him which such thunderous applause because it suggested they were pleased that his would-be-assassins had failed.

Once the speeches had been given, Franz Ferdinand and his entourage convened inside the Town Hall to discuss what they should do next. Baron Rumerskirch, one of the Archduke's friends, suggested that the best course of action, in case there were more assassins present, would be to sit tight inside the Town Hall until a force of soldiers could be brought in from outside town to line the streets and allow them to make their egress with appropriate security. However, this eminently sensible suggestion was rejected by Governor Potiorek, who insisted that since the soldiers would be returning from the maneuvers that Franz Ferdinand had previously witnessed, they would be travel-stained and in field attire rather than parade uniform, thus making them unfit to bodyguard royalty. Although understandably upset at the situation, Franz Ferdinand ultimately agreed with Sophie that the best course of action would be to leave the Town Hall, if only to show his entourage and the inhabitants of Sarajevo that he was unafraid.

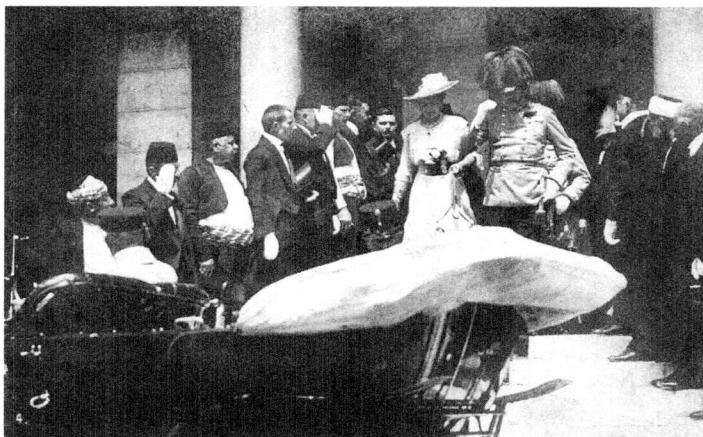

A picture of the Archduke and Sophie leaving Town Hall

Accordingly, the motorcade departed Town Hall around 10:45 to head for the hospital where the victims of the bombing had been taken so that the Archduke and his wife could pay their respects, but the trouble started almost immediately. Colonel von Harrach, the Archduke's military advisor, took up station next to Franz Ferdinand and stood on the car's running board rather than inside in order to shelter him from any shooters, but that was the last practical notion those in charge of the convoy displayed. Governor Potiorek felt that the safest route would be to avoid the city center entirely and proceed along the riverbank to the hospital, but other than the Governor himself, no one knew about this change of plan. With Potiorek's aide in the hospital, he delegated the task of informing the motorcade's drivers to the Chief of the Sarajevo Police, who promptly forgot to tell any of the drivers. The convoy thus abandoned the river route and turned into the crowded city center, where Princip and Grabež were still lurking.

As the convoy turned off the riverbank, Potiorek, located in the Archduke's car, shouted at the drivers to stop because he wanted them to take the safer route, but this resulted in bringing the motorcade to a complete halt. As fate would have it, the motorcade stopped just feet away from where Princip was lurking near the Latin Bridge. The driver fussed with the gears in order to put the car in reverse, and with the vehicles at a dead stop, Princip realized that it was now or never to make an attempt. He stepped forward, drew the Model 1910 from under his coat, and fired just two shots. To his credit, Princip did not panic or madly empty the pistol into the car, and his aim proved true. The first bullet struck the Archduke in the neck, causing him to jerk back and thus expose Sophie. According to his testimony, Princip's second shot was off the mark, perhaps because of the weapon's recoil and his lack of training. The assassin claimed that instead of hitting his intended target, Governor Potiorek, he inadvertently shot Sophie in the chest. Whether that's true or not remains unclear, as Princip may well have changed his story in order to appear more sympathetic to the jury (political assassination could be understood if not condoned, whereas shooting defenseless women would be unlikely to win him any supporters).

Contemporary media depiction of the assassination

A picture of the gun Princip used to shoot the Archduke

Princip had no chance to make his escape even if he had wanted to, and he was unable to use his cyanide pill. Within seconds, bystanders and police officials tackled him to the ground and wrestled the pistol away from him, but by then it was too late.

A picture of Princip after being arrested

Incredibly, in the immediate aftermath of the shooting, the convoy began to speed away from the scene of Princip's attack to foil any other assassins, yet nobody realized that the Archduke and Sophie had been hit. It was only when Franz Ferdinand suddenly coughed blood into Colonel von Harrach's face that the colonel understood what had happened. With a cry of horror, he tried to loosen the Archduke's jacket to get at the wound, but he was unable to do so; the stiff, double-breasted military coat, which was soaking with blood, needed to be cut open. Von Harrach seized his handkerchief and attempted to staunch the flow of blood, but it was a hopeless battle because the bullet had torn the Archduke's jugular, which was now beginning to pump blood in vast quantities down his front. Seeing the blood, Sophie cried out and tried to reach for Franz Ferdinand, only to slump forward onto his lap. Von Harrach, bellowing that the Archduke was hurt and for the convoy to make for the hospital at the quickest possible speed as he clung to the car's side, assumed that she had fainted with shock, but Franz Ferdinand knew what had happened. He tried to raise her despite his own wound in an attempt to staunch the blood that was soaking through her dress and dripping onto the floor of the car. The Archduke called out to her, imploring her not to die so that she could live for their children, but this effort taxed him so much that he slumped into the car seat, his head rolling backwards. Von Harrach asked the Archduke whether he was in much pain, and the Archduke simply replied, "It is nothing. It is nothing."

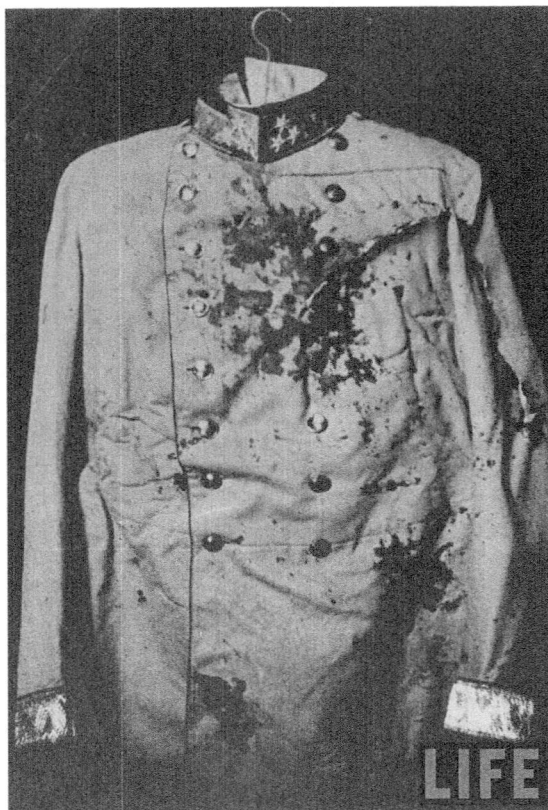

Picture of the Archduke's bloody jacket

A contemporary account captured the moments after the assassination in detail:

"One bullet pierced Franz Ferdinand's neck while the other pierced Sophie's abdomen. ... As the car was reversing (to go back to the Governor's residence because the entourage thought the Imperial couple were unhurt) a thin streak of blood shot from the Archduke's mouth onto Count Harrach's right cheek (he was standing on the car's running board). Harrach drew out a handkerchief to still the gushing blood. The Duchess, seeing this, called: 'For Heaven's sake! What happened to you?' and sank from her seat, her face falling between her husband's knees.

Harrach and Potoriek ... thought she had fainted ... only her husband seemed to have an instinct for what was happening. Turning to his wife despite the bullet in his neck, Franz Ferdinand pleaded: 'Sopherl! Sopherl! Sterbe nicht! Bleibe am Leben für unsere Kinder! - Sophie dear! Don't die! Stay alive for our children!' Having said this, he seemed to sag down himself. His plumed hat ... fell off, many of its green feathers were found all over the car floor. Count Harrach seized the Archduke by the uniform collar to hold him up. He asked 'Leiden Eure Kaiserliche Hoheit sehr? - Is Your Imperial Highness suffering very badly?' 'Es ist nichts. - It is nothing.' said the Archduke in a weak but audible voice. He seemed to be losing consciousness during his last few minutes, but, his voice growing steadily weaker, he repeated the phrase perhaps six or seven times more.

A rattle began to issue from his throat, which subsided as the car drew in front of the Konak bersibin (Town Hall). Despite several doctors' efforts, the Archduke died shortly after being carried into the building while his beloved wife was almost certainly dead from internal bleeding before the motorcade reached the Konak."

Several doctors rushed to attend him, but it was too late. Sophie herself had never regained consciousness after calling out to her husband, and in all likelihood she bled out before the convoy reached the Town Hall. The Archduke and his wife were dead. They were buried together, in accordance with their wishes, in Arstetten Castle in Austria, alongside one of their children who had not survived infancy.

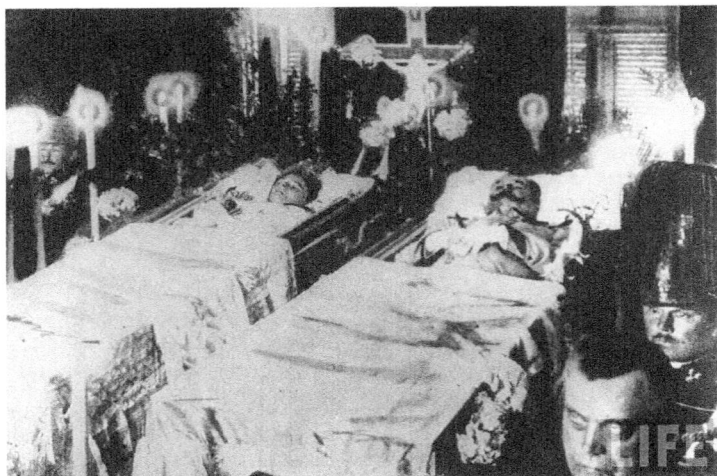

Pictures of the funeral

New York Times **headline**

In the wake of the assassination, the Sarajevo police were mobilized on an unprecedented scale, with the army in support, and a veritable witch hunt began. Princip and Čabrinović were already in custody, and they apparently confessed (most likely under torture) the details of the conspiracy because all of the would-be-assassins were eventually arrested, along with Ilic himself and those members of the Black Hand and People's Defence who had abetted the assassins' journey across the border to Austria-Hungary. Surprisingly, the hapless Mehmedbasic managed to escape to Montenegro, where he was finally taken into custody, but then – under very suspicious circumstances – he managed to escape from the police and make his way back to Serbia, where he was taken in by Major Tankosic.

Franz Ferdinand and Sophie had been fairly popular figures, but the fact that the assassination had been perpetrated by Serbs seemingly acting in collusion with that country's government truly riled the loyal Austro-Hungarians within the borders of the empire. Despite the tense situation between the two countries, thousands of Serbs still lived in Sarajevo, throughout Bosnia, and even further afield, and those Serb citizens, peaceful and law-abiding and likely abhorrent of violence though they might be, suddenly found themselves under attack. Word of the Archduke's murder spread like wildfire throughout Austria-Hungary, and widespread rioting broke out in several cities. Sarajevo, as the location of the Archduke's death and the city with the largest number of Serbs living within it, saw the worst violence, not least because Governor Potoriek helped instigate the riots and then did nothing to mitigate them when they inevitably got out of hand. Over the next two days, the Serbs in the city were subjected to an organized campaign of hate. A great many were severely beaten, regardless of age or sex, and two young men who tried to fight back were killed outright by the mob. Any buildings that were suspected of belonging to Serbs were ransacked, burned, or torn down stone by stone. This did not merely include commercial properties but also private homes, schools, and churches. Many families were left entirely destitute, with all of their belongings either stolen or destroyed along with their homes.

A picture of anti-Serb rioters on June 29

Once the violence had subsided and all the suspects except Mehmedbasic were in custody, the official proceedings could begin. Unsurprisingly, given the circumstances, the trial went ahead with the minimum possible amount of delay, and within days, charges of conspiracy to commit high treason were brought. This was a severe blow to the hopes of the conspirators, especially those who were not directly involved in the assassination attempt and were in all likelihood not ready to be martyrs, because conspiracy to commit murder was not punishable by death under

Austro-Hungarian law but conspiracy to commit high treason was. The trial began in Sarajevo less than four months after Franz Ferdinand was killed, and it lasted for 11 days.

Five days after the end of the trial, exactly four months to the day of the assassination, the sentences were announced. In the meantime, a spell in prison apparently dampened the conspirators' ardor for a glorious death in the name of Serbian hegemony. Clearly operating in collusion with the other defendants, Princip, Čabrinović and Grabež, who were under the age of 20 and thus minors according to Austro-Hungarian law (which meant that they could not be sentenced to death), shouldered the lion's share of the blame. Princip, as might be expected from the man who had struck the fatal blow against Franz Ferdinand, was the most vocal of the conspirators. He declared himself a Yugoslav nationalist fighting for the cause of Slavic unification in whatever form, so long as it was free of Austrian interference. When he was asked how he intended to achieve that goal, his answer was simple: terror.

Čabrinović and Grabež had similar, if more moderate views, which also attempted to exculpate the Serbian government, the Black Hand and the People's Defence from any blame. Čabrinović, in his testimony, claimed that he had been influenced by popularly held views in Serbia, but that he and the other two had acted alone with little or no help from any others and certainly no official support, arms or training from the Serbian government. Čabrinović also expressed regret for what he had done, and he claimed that he would not act similarly again if he were offered the chance. This was in stark contrast to Princip, who appeared proud and unrepentant. Franz Ferdinand's children later wrote Čabrinović a letter while he was in prison in which they expressed their forgiveness.

Pictures of the trial with Princip front and center

The court, however, was not buying any suggested regret on the parts of the defendants. When they heard the stories of the other defendants, who were all old enough to be tried as adults and thus at risk of the death penalty, the whole web began to unravel. Veljko Cubrilovic (not to be confused with Vaso Cubrilovic, the would-be-assassin who was apparently no relation), a member of the People's Defence who had helped Princip and Grabež move to Tuzla, claimed that when he had questioned Princip and the others as to their motives, Princip had explained that they intended to murder Franz Ferdinand, and that if he valued his life and his family's he would keep quiet and cooperate. Cubrilovic pleaded with the court that he had been coerced into acting against his will because of the threat to his family's life, begging them for leniency. Nonetheless, the court was disinclined to be merciful, which was understandable given what was at stake. Despite the declarations of the defendants, sufficient evidence had been collected to satisfy the court that the Serbian government had been up to its neck in the whole sordid affair. The official verdict read, "The court believes it to be manifestly proven that the People's Defence and the Military Espionage Services of the Kingdom of Serbia were jointly responsible for the atrocity."

Naturally, the Austro-Hungarians were hardly prepared to be merciful either. Gavrilo Princip, Nedjelko Čabrinović and Trifun Grabež received 20 years' imprisonment apiece, the maximum allowable sentence given that they were all minors, and while that might sound better than the death penalty, the jails were notoriously unsanitary and miserable places. Ultimately, both Princip and Čabrinović contracted tuberculosis in prison and died within a few years. Vaso Cubrilovic and Cvjetko Popovic, the two Black Hand members recruited by Danilo Ilic who failed to attack the Archduke's motorcade, were given 16 years and 13 years respectively. Ilic and Veljko Cubrilovic, who had pleaded so desperately for his life, were both sentenced to death by hanging, the usual punishment for treason. The two of them were executed along with a third member of the conspiracy, Mihailo Jovanovic, on February 3, 1915. Nedjo Kerovic and Jakov Milovic, members of the People's Defence, were also sentenced to death, but Kaiser Wilhelm commuted their sentences to 20 years and life in prison respectively. Another half a dozen defendants were given varying prison sentences ranging from 3-13 years in prison, and 9 others were acquitted of all wrongdoing.

Another, far less equitable trial (if such a term can be used to describe something which was, from a judicial standpoint, a virtual farce) took place in Salonika in the spring of 1917, when World War I was already in its third year. Millions had already died, countless more had seen their lives destroyed, and Austria was weary of fighting, increasingly friendless, and seeking a way out of the fight. Accordingly, Austrian diplomats held secret talks in the early months of that year with French foreign office agents, and also with representatives of the Serbian Prime Minister, Pasic, and the Regent of the Kingdom, Crown Prince Alexander. The Serbian government was languishing in exile, but Charles I, who had succeeded Franz Joseph I as Emperor of Austria, stated that he was willing to hand control of the country back to its legitimate rulers provided that Serbia desist from its campaign of sabotage and rabble-rousing within Austro-Hungarian borders.

This suited Alexander and the Serbian government in exile perfectly, as it also afforded them the opportunity to rid themselves of Dimitrijević, who continued to act in his capacity as head of the Serbian Military Intelligence and was as vicious and malevolent as ever despite losing his right-hand man, Vojislav Tankosic, in battle against the Austrians in the autumn of 1915. Plans were laid and set in motion, and in mid-March 1917, Dimitrijević and his closest associates were captured and imprisoned. Among them was Mehmedbasic, who after escaping to Serbia had joined the Secret Police under Dimitrijević's instructions. In all, 12 men were brought to trial and tried by a Serbian military court martial in Salonika, where the French technically had nominal control. The charges brought were trumped up and unrelated to the events in Sarajevo, but only members of Military Intelligence who were either thought to have directly been involved in the operation or were unfortunate enough to be members of Dimitrijević's inner circle were accused. Of those tried, 9 were sentenced to death, 2 received 15 years of hard labor (including Mehmedbasic, who was released in 1919, making him by far the luckiest of the original conspirators), and 1 died during the trial under mysterious circumstances. Of those sentenced to death, two were reprieved by the court and a further four were pardoned by Alexander. The three who were to face the firing squad with no possibility of appeal were Dimitrijević, Rade Malobabic, and Ljuba Vulovic. All three were executed on June 26, 1917, with Dimitrijević remarking on the way to the esplanade where he would meet his end that he was obviously being punished not for the charges brought against him at Salonika but because he had masterminded the death of Franz Ferdinand.

The trial was obviously a farce, so much so that when the Serbian Supreme Court famously organized a retrial of the 12 defendants, they exonerated all 12 of the charges for those particular crimes. Of course, what they would have made of Dimitrijević, Malobabic and Vulovic's involvement in the death of Franz Ferdinand is another matter, but either way, it was patently obvious that Dimitrijević was being railroaded for what he had instigated at Sarajevo, so much so that Prime Minister Pasic even wrote in an official letter that Dimitrijević had confessed to ordering the death of Franz Ferdinand and in light of what followed, he could never be forgiven.

Chapter 6: Reaping the Whirlwind

The world reacted with horror to the death of Franz Ferdinand and Sophie, nowhere more so than throughout Austria-Hungary, where there was widespread rioting against innocent Serbian citizens living within the empire's borders. It is surmised that many of those displaced eventually made their way back across the border to Serbia as refugees, further inflaming sentiment against Austrians and making an already volatile situation that much worse. Expressions of horror and commiseration came in from Germany, France, Britain (although the public and the government's attention there were far more focused on the rapidly escalating crisis in Ireland, where the independence movement had turned violent), and even Austria's recent enemy, Italy. Russia also offered its condolences, which was quite hypocritical given that the Russian government was almost certainly aware of the Serbian plot.

Overwhelmingly, the Great Powers sided with Austria, and a joint Austro-Hungarian and German demand was presented to the Serbian government to commence an internal investigation into the assassination, but the Serbian Ministry of Foreign Affairs dismissed such a request out of hand, claiming that there was absolutely nothing to investigate. This further aggravated an already awkward situation.

In the wake of the investigation into the death of Franz Ferdinand and the resulting trial and sentences that followed, along with the verdict of the court inculpating Serbia for the murders, the Austro-Hungarian Empire ultimately issued a letter to Serbia which became known as the July Ultimatum. This inflammatory letter demanded that the Kingdom of Serbia repudiate in writing the acts of the terrorists intent on destabilizing the legitimacy of the Austro-Hungarian monarchy and their hold over Bosnia-Herzegovina, and it also reminded the Serbian government that it had bound itself to abide by the terms of the agreement ceding it to Austria-Hungary in the first place. The letter also listed 10 key points which Serbia was expected to accept within 48 hours, and it threatened retaliation in the case of non-compliance.

The points listed were as follows:

    1.   Serbia must renounce all propaganda designed to inspire hatred towards Austria-Hungary and which might prove harmful to its territorial integrity.

    2.   The Organization known as the People's Defence must be disbanded forthwith, along with all organizations of a similar ilk.

    3.   All propaganda against Austria-Hungary published in public documents, including school textbooks, is to be eliminated forthwith.

    4.   All officers and government officials named by the Austro-Hungarian government are to be removed from office immediately.

    5.   Members of the Austro-Hungarian government will be dispatched immediately to Belgrade, where they are to be given every assistance in suppressing subversive movements.

    6.   All those involved in Franz Ferdinand's assassination are to be brought to trial forthwith, with the assistance of police investigators from Austria-Hungary.

    7.   Major Vojislav Tankosic and Milan Ciganovic, known participants in the assassination of the royal couple, are to be immediately arrested.

8.   The Serbian government must cease all collusion in the transportation of weapons and equipment across the Austro-Hungarian Border, dismissing and disciplining the Border Patrol officials at Sabac and Loznica, who abetted the Sarajevo conspirators.

9.   Provide suitable explanation to the Austro-Hungarian government with regards to the actions undertaken by certain Serbian officials, who have demonstrated an attitude of hostility in their negotiations with the Austrian government.

10.   Immediately notify the Austro-Hungarian government once these measures have been enacted.

The letter set off a frantic flurry of activity in Serbia, but not of the kind the Austro-Hungarians wanted, aside from those in office who were clearly spoiling for a fight. Serbia telegraphed to St Petersburg asking for support, which Russia promised in the event of a fight. Reassured, Serbia then mobilized its armed forces before sending a reply to the July Ultimatum that conceded both points 8 and 10 but rejected the remaining points. The Serbs disguised their explicit refusal with a wealth of diplomatic actions that did nothing to fool the Austro-Hungarian government. The response from the empire was swift; the Austro-Hungarian ambassador in Belgrade was recalled, and troops began to prepare in for mobilization.

A propaganda cartoon after the assassination that asserted "Serbia must die!"

The day after the Austro-Hungarian ambassador departed from Belgrade, a convoy of Serbian troops being transported down the Danube River by steamer drifted off course towards the Austro-Hungarian bank near Temes-Kubin, where the local garrison commander ordered shots fired into the air to discourage them from landing. He wisely avoided firing upon the boats, which might well have precipitated a full-scale crisis, but as it was, his level-headedness would be to no avail. Unfortunately, the report which reached Emperor Franz Joseph I in Vienna about this incident inaccurately portrayed the trifling affair as a bloody last-ditch skirmish, and Franz Joseph I responded by declaring war. The Austrian Army was brought forward to a state of full mobilization, and the allotted divisions moved forward to their position on the Serbian border.

This was the move that set the dominoes of war in motion. Russia and France immediately mobilized their armies in response to the Austro-Hungarian threat, as they were required to do so according to the terms of the Secret Treaty of 1892, which stated that any mobilization of members of the Triple Alliance must be met. The initial, limited mobilization by Austria-Hungary was followed by a full-scale Russian one, which in turn was followed by a full-scale German and Austro-Hungarian call-up, which in turn precipitated a French one and finally a British one. Thus, with a suddenness that startled even those who felt it was inevitable, the major European powers all found themselves at war.

Although there had been explicit displays of commiseration and sympathy for Austria and widespread condemnation of Serbia's actions in the immediate aftermath of Franz Ferdinand's assassination, the attitude of the great powers towards Austria as the notional aggrieved party became substantially chillier as Austria insisted on virtually bullying Serbia over the whole affair. The British Prime Minister, Asquith, complained in an official letter that Serbia had no hope of appeasing Austria diplomatically, and that the terms of the July Ultimatum would've been impossible to meet even if Serbia was willing to do so. Indeed, it appears as though such an exacting document had been drafted precisely because Serbia didn't have a hope of complying, even if they had so wished, and thus Austria-Hungary would be able to go to war and punish them properly for the outrage perpetrated against their royal family.

100 years removed from the assassination, it might be unfair to say that it caused World War I, but it certainly started it. Historians still debate whether the Great War would have occurred even if Franz Ferdinand and Sophie lived out their lives in peace and comfort, but many believe that while it might've come months or years down the road, it was inevitable. The tangled web of alliances at cross-purposes, the growing diplomatic tensions, the arms race, the belligerence of newly powerful states such as Germany, the interference in other sovereign countries' affairs, and the relentless politicking all pointed towards one tragic outcome.

As for the parties themselves, it's apparent that much of the blame can be shouldered by the Serbian government. To this day, it's still unclear how much the King and Prime Minister knew about the plots and actions carried out by Dimitrijević and his associates in the Black Hand, but they were obviously privy to the official communications that involved Dimitrijević in his capacity as the head of Serbian Military Intelligence. Furthermore, it was the Serbian government, not the Black Hand (which at that point was virtually synonymous with Dimitrijević and Military Intelligence in any case) that provided Princip, Grabež, Cubrilovic, and the other conspirators with their firearms, explosives, training, and the means to cross the border into Bosnia. The People's Defence, the clandestine group within Bosnia, had been almost completely taken over by Serbian Military Intelligence and was effectively acting as a shell organization. Government officials from several different agencies had colluded with the conspirators on many occasions, with the end result that on the day of the assassination, the assassins were in place, suitably organized, well-armed for their purpose, and ready for action. At the same time, there are strong indications that several officials within the Serbian government (with or without sanction from on high) attempted to warn their Austro-Hungarian counterparts of what was to come.

Another country that must bear a share of the blame is Russia. According to the confession given by Dimitrijević at the end of his 1917 trial in Salonika, Russia was fully aware of his activities, and he had no reason to lie at that point. Indeed, according to Dimitrijević, the Russian Military Attachè in Belgrade had guaranteed that Russia would stand with Serbia against Austria-Hungary in the event that the operation was compromised, and that he had received funds from Russia to carry out the assassination. An investigative journalist attempting to uncover the truth received a fairly unconvincing testimony from the Russian Military Attachè, who denied any involvement. The Russian Military Attachè claimed that his Assistant had been in charge during the period leading up to the assassination, and that Dimitrijević never apprised him of his plans or intentions. It has also been suggested that the Tsar, or at the very least the Prime Minister, were aware of a forthcoming attempt against Franz Ferdinand's life and were not opposed to it happening. Russia had a vested interest both in weakening the Austro-Hungarian Empire and in destabilizing its hold on the Balkans as this might well potentially give it access to the strategically invaluable Mediterranean ports without having to pass through the Turkish-controlled Bosphorus and Dardanelles straits, which hampered its attempts to increase its naval power outside of the Black Sea.

Even Austria-Hungary, despite being the aggrieved party, had a hand in what followed the assassination. The Austro-Hungarian military had resisted many attempts at pacification with Serbia, including policies advocated by Franz Ferdinand himself, and it continued to pursue a policy of aggressive saber-rattling. Furthermore, the Governor of Bosnia, Oskar Potiorek, was a rigid and stubborn individual who viewed Slavic patriots as a national security threat and ruthlessly punished them accordingly, further inflaming anti-Austrian sentiment in a newly created province that required the most delicate of management rather than hamfisted pacification attempts. His refusal to countenance the use of improperly dressed troops to shield Franz Ferdinand and his halting of the motorcade in a vulnerable position near the bank of the river were symptomatic of his stubbornness, and his decision to remain idle while Sarajevo tore apart the homes of hundreds of innocent Serbs is evidence of his poor character.

Ironically, one of the few people who had no blame in what was to come was Franz Ferdinand himself. A choleric individual with the typical Austrian aristocrat's condescending attitude towards the subordinate Hungarian population, he was nonetheless no more prejudiced than many during his time and a great deal less than most; after all, he married a woman from the Czech aristocracy who was beneath his station. On top of that, his attitude towards Serbia and the Slavic issue was remarkably conciliatory for someone in his position. He went to his death unwittingly even after bravely continuing his public appearance despite having a hand grenade hurled at him. It is unfortunate for Franz Ferdinand that his birth and position made him an ideal target, but as history and fate would have it, he was simply the right man in the wrong place at the wrong time.

Bibliography

Albertini, Luigi (2005). Origins of the War of 1914 I. New York: Enigma Books. ISBN 1-929631-31-6.

Dedijer, Vladimir (1966). The Road to Sarajevo. New York: Simon and Schuster. OCLC 400010.

Fay, Sidney Bradshaw: Origins of the Great War. New York 1928

MacKenzie, David (1995). Black Hand on Trial: Salonika 1917. Eastern European Monographs. ISBN 978-0-88033-320-7.

Owings, W.A. Dolph. (1984). The Sarajevo Trial. Chapel Hill, NC.: Documentary Publications. ISBN 0-89712-122-8.

Ponting, Clive. Thirteen Days, Chatto & Windus, London, 2002.

Stoessinger, John. Why Nations Go to War, Wadsworth Publishing, 2007.

Donia, Robert J. (2006). Sarajevo: A Biography. University of Michigan Press. ISBN 978-0-472-11557-0.

Johnson, Wes (2007). Balkan Inferno: Betrayal, War and Intervention, 1990-2005. Enigma Books. ISBN 978-1-929631-63-6.

Mitrović, Andrej (2007). Serbia's Great War, 1914–1918. Purdue University Press. ISBN 978-1-55753-477-4.

Strachan, Hugh (2001). The First World War. I: To Arms. Oxford: Oxford University Press. ISBN 978-0-19-926191-8.

Remak, Joachim (1971). The First World War: Causes, Conduct, Consequences. Wiley. ISBN 0-471-71634-0.

MacKenzie, David (1989). Apis, the Congenial Conspirator: the Life of Colonel Dragutin T. Dimitrijević. East European Monographs.

Printed in Great Britain
by Amazon